Stuck in a Cave

I0814010

BY KIM THOMPSON

A Little Honey Book

Tips for Teachers and Caregivers

This book supports early readers as they decode words to learn facts and gain knowledge about the world.

Before reading, make sure students understand the sound-spelling correspondences shown below as well as the high-frequency words shown on the next page. Introduce the vocabulary words.

During reading, provide feedback and encouragement as students sound out decodable words by blending individual sounds.

After reading, talk about and write about the topic. Share the information on page 16 to help students learn more.

Letters and Sounds

New:

none

Review:

all consonant sounds and standard spellings; consonant digraphs *sh* and *th* (voiceless); *short a* spelled *a*, *short e* spelled *e*, *short i* spelled *i*, *short o* spelled *o*, *short u* spelled *u*

Decodable Words

short a: and, as, black, drank, gaps, glad, had, map, masks, path, plan, ran, sat, swam, tanks, trap

short e: help, led, met, rest, well, went

short i: did, grin, him, in, it, kids, quick, swim, trips, wish

short o: block, drops, got, lots, not, on, rocks, spot

short u: fun, luck, lug, mud, pumps, rush, stuck, suck, up

High-Frequency Words

New: boys, came, nine, through, took, were, would

Review: a, all, cold, days, find, for, from, live, made, of, one, out, people, saw, see, some, the, their, them, they, to, was, water, where

Vocabulary Words

cave

divers

news

ropes

statue

team

In 2018, a **team** met for fun.

12 boys went in a **cave**. They saw water rush in and block their path. They got stuck.

The spot where they sat was a trap. It was cold. It was black. The kids drank drops from rocks. They had to rest.

Divers came to help.

They made a cave map.

They ran **ropes** through gaps. It took nine days to find the kids.

People made a plan.

Pumps would suck up some water and mud.

Divers would lug in masks and tanks. They would help the kids swim.

Ropes led the kids as they swam. Divers made lots of trips.

People saw it on the **news**. They made a wish for luck.

news

LIVE
BREAKING NEWS
THAI CAVE BOYS GOING HOME
Boys to take part in news conference shortly
BBC WORLD NEWS
BAY HOTEL OWNER SUES 1,000 VICTIMS

statue

All the kids got out. They got well quick. People were glad to see them grin.

One diver did not live. A **statue** was made for him.

Build Background Knowledge

In 2018, people around the world held their breath when news broke that a Thai soccer team, the Wild Boars, was trapped more than two miles (three kilometers) inside a flooded cave system during monsoon season. Stranded were 12 boys ages 11 to 16 along with their coach. It took an international team nine days to find the group and another eight days to rescue them. Learning about historical events like this one helps people understand how complex situations unfold over time. A variety of sources, including text and photographs, provide multiple viewpoints.

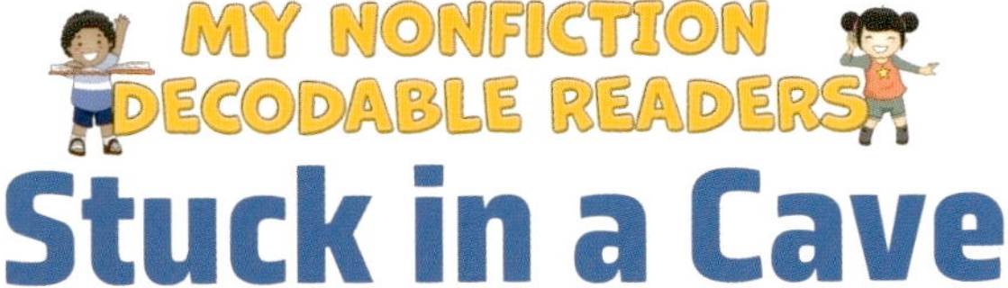

Stuck in a Cave

Written by: Kim Thompson
Designed by: Rhea Magaro
Series Development: James Earley
Educational Consultant: Marie Lemke, M.Ed.

Photographs: All images from Shutterstock

Crabtree Publishing

crabtreebooks.com 800-387-7650

Copyright © 2025 Crabtree Publishing

All rights reserved. No part of this publication may be reproduced, stored in a retrieval system or be transmitted in any form or by any means, electronic, mechanical, photocopying, recording, or otherwise, without the prior written permission of Crabtree Publishing.

Printed in China/012024/FE20231222

Published in Canada
Crabtree Publishing
616 Welland Ave.
St. Catharines, Ontario
L2M 5V6

Published in the United States
Crabtree Publishing
347 Fifth Ave
Suite 1402-145
New York, NY 10016

Library and Archives Canada Cataloguing in Publication
Available at Library and Archives Canada

Library of Congress Cataloging-in-Publication Data
Available at the Library of Congress

Hardcover: 978-1-0398-4443-8
Paperback: 978-1-0398-4524-4
Ebook (pdf): 978-1-0398-4601-2
Epub: 978-1-0398-4671-5
Read-Along: 978-1-0398-4741-5
Audio: 978-1-0398-4811-5